Being ME

Kavya Chakraborty

Invincible Publishers

First published in India in 2019

ISBN: 978-93-88333-92-4

Registered Address: 201A, SAS Tower, Sector 38,
Gurgaon-122003

Printed at Thomson Press (India) LTD

In the book I am using both the names of my daughter, mainly because she was known to many as Mishti and as Kavya to many others.

Even before she was born, her brother chose Mishti (meaning 'sweets' in Bangla) as the *daak naam* (pet name), in case he was being blessed with a sister. And, then we thought of naming her Kavya as her official name. Her poetic fervour talks the rest.

She lived both names to the fullest. Most Bengalis who met her often said, *'Mishti, tumi shotti khub mishti'*.

Preface

This book is a collection of poems written by my daughter, Kavya Chakraborty, who was fondly called Mishti. These poems are written by her over a span of 11 months, starting October 2017. She has recited some of these poems and won prizes in open mic events. She was also invited as guest artist in several spoken word poetry events held in Delhi & NCR during this time. Her prowess for writing shaped up when she was in her primary classes. She started writing short poems, short stories and journals when she was in her 3rd standard. At a very young age she had well-formed opinions about society, relationships and her aspirations. Most of her poems are the product of her powerful imagination, near real experiences, her struggles and the current state of society, all combined with her creativity.

No one knows how life is going to treat us but surely, death is inevitable. The way life came to an end for my daughter is most ghastly and painful. In no time it engulfed her and left me numb with shock. All that I am left with is an ocean of memories, her unfinished dreams and regrets hovering over me.

She was declared to be bipolar and suffering from borderline personality disorder & depression in the middle of 2017. She was receiving treatment but perhaps not everything worked well in her case. As we were together in this journey, I found there are people like her in this world who are suffering from one or more of these mental disorders. This book is also to help everyone like her (and their immediate circle of influence) who are struggling to find their place in this world. Do what it takes to be with them and understand them because all is not enough. I wish them all well and I will be happy to share my experiences if it can help them understand their situations better.

Through her art in the form of this book I am trying to connect all of us to her, thus making an attempt to keep her and the art in her alive; a connection perhaps made better. The poems are collected from her blogs, handwritten notes and her journals. Her poems and the snippets written by people in her loving memory may be able to convey her persona. Yes, that's her. I miss her terribly, beyond any expression.

I am grateful to people, who took out time amidst their busy schedule to contribute to this memoir and sent me their thoughts like "Flash" (An analogy Mishti would always refer to). These memoirs are my treasure!

My heartfelt thanks to all the people especially Mishti's friends and mine who supported me in making this book a reality. Also, I could not start working on it until my son, Shrey joined me. He is my armour. I had aimed to get this book published on Mishti's 1st anniversary and without all of you it would not have been possible. A special mention to my editing buddy, Akriti, my daughter's friend who willingly took to help me when she also had her serious studies going on and still asking if she can help in any other way. It might have been so painful for her to go through each of the poems and snippets. I feel sorry for making her go through these emotionally tiring moments.

I take a moment to express my gratitude to Sengupta ma'am for the special guidance & encouragement given to me from time to time. Anuja's suggestions for the cover page is the most perfect. Thank you Anuja! My special thanks to Anushka, Noel, Rudraaksh and Astha. Your visits, contributions and support during the book writing phase has been heart-warming. Tons of thanks to Nidhi and Daisy for their untiring support and comforting words, always!

I take this as an opportunity to especially thank the therapist, doctors, teachers, my seniors, colleagues, friends and family who have supported me in all possible ways then and now. Thank you very much! My special thanks to those who have been my support all through the last several months, calling me, visiting me and making sure to spend time with me on their travel to India. It gives me better moments. I will forever remain indebted to all of you.

It is important to connect to a good publisher especially when expressions are very high on emotions. My sincere thanks and gratitude to my publisher. All these times Ajay & his team treated me very generously and extended all possible support, especially at times when it has been difficult for me to express my thoughts on why I want to do certain things in a particular way. All these times he treated me like no one else could!

My special thanks to my friend, Tarun for suggesting the most understanding and compassionate publisher, "Invincible Publishers".

I hope Kavya's poems and the book will touch your heart.

In the loving memory of my daughter, Mishti
I do, miss you, a whole lot.
Leena Chakraborty

"And now my bitter hands cradle broken glass,
Of what was everything.
All the pictures have all been washed in black,
Tattooed everything.

All the love gone bad turned my world to black
Tattooed all I see, all that I am, all I'll be."

I think I had a very surreal relation with my sister. We would mostly tease each other and pick up fights over everything, whether a piece of kebab or a slice of pizza or the last block of chocolate. Mum had a tough time dividing things between us. Sometimes I would be the triumphant one and at others, she.

All my winnings seem so meagre now. Everything remains the same except that I've already won all the fights and all spoils are already mine.

All the memories of these fights (physical and verbal) and the spats still have a raw memory but sadly What is a victor without the one over whom he had his victory? Your loss has put me into an existential crisis. It is like Batman without Joker, Tom without Jerry; Me without You.

The above lyrics are from a song called 'Black' by Pearl Jam which is based on unrequited love. I used to listen to the song in the same light until you left. After which, all the love has gone bad and it has turned my life into memories of you inked in Black.

Bones

You tell me I love
a little too much,
a little too hard.
But isn't that what love is?
–a little bit of all the 'toos'?
You tell me I am not normal;
not normal enough for you.
But isn't that something
that sets me apart?
–my abnormality; as you call it?
I told you–
"You are my angel".
Little did I know,
that not all angels take you to heaven.
Some take you
straight back to hell.
I told you,
you were my saving grace.
But, in time,
all you did was ruin me,
over and over again.
They told me–
"Don't get too attached".
But, I saw love and

all I did was, jump
– jump right into it.
What I didn't realize was
that I jumped without a parachute.
Now, when I see you,
coming at me,
from across the room,
I stare at you
with my broken limbs.
And that's when it hit me
–just like my shattered bones
cannot possibly grow again,
my love for you, cannot either.
And so, I apologize and leave.

- kc

Kavya, as her name suggests is poetry. Everybody doesn't understand the art of poetry. You have to rise high in intellectualism and beyond the shackles of society to know her. She was deep as a person and I feel grateful to have met her. I have learned a lot from her and I miss her. I still remember the last time I saw her and we connected there. I remember her as a person who could speak from her eyes. I am sure wherever she is, she is glowing the best among all.

Ms. Alisha Arora
Clinical Psychologist

Static

As I stand under the shower
and feel the hot water
running down my body,
I gaze at the water droplets
as they pour down
and I...
I think to myself,
why am I not like it?
Why I am not consistent?
Why am I not persistent?
But then, I realize,
–I'm not static,
I am like the waves,
I come and go.
I move at my own pace.
And yes, I keep changing
my pace. So?
I am like the thunders
you cannot predict would arrive
but, when they do,
you are taken aback.
I am dysfunctional, yes.
I am dysfunctional,
but in a beautiful way.

Hello? I have bipolar disorder.
I am not static.
And I will never be,
Nor do I want to be.
I am the surprise gift,
on a Sunday morning,
making you smile all
through the week.
I am the hangover after a
bad night of too much of whiskey,
the one you hate the next
morning but would come back
to. Or, at least, savour
memories of.
On some days,
I will fill your ears
with my ridiculous stories.
And on others?
You will fall
in love with my silence.
On some days,
you will hate me.
On other days,
you won't be able to
stop loving me.
They say there are always
two sides to a story,
two sides of a coin;
here I am–two people in one;

I'm not static, nor will i ever be

two extremes in one.
I turn the knob,
and the shower
slowly stops pouring water.
And there, then,
I am reminded, I am not like the water
which pours out of my shower,
because,
I am so much more than
consistent. I am a new
tomorrow, everyday.
No, I am not static.
And I am proud not to be.

- kc

Kavya Chakraborty, a very passionate and confident poet, inspired many by her words and thoughtfulness. We're really grateful that she's been a part of our community.

Safarnama Words & Melody

Was it?

Was it easy for you
to take the final call?
Or were you just as
devastated as I am
after knowing your
decision?
Was it you,
who made the choice?
Or was it under
someone else's influence?
Because day and night,
I wish and pray it's the latter.
Was it easy for you
to choose black and white
over all the colours
I was willing to offer you?
Or is black and white all you've
ever wanted from your life?
Was it easy for you
to leave because you knew you'd find
yourself in most of my writings
if not all.
Or did you leave,
because you never wanted to be

a part of my writings to begin with?
Would you ever come back?
Or are my poems the only place
where I'd find you?

- kc

Heartbreak

They say
if you have a heart,
heartbreak isn't too far away.
They say
don't be attached to anyone
because when they leave,
a part of your soul leaves too.
But I came too close to you
to not be attached
and eventually,
you left.
Leaving me alone
with the thoughts of you
and a reminder
that you'd never come back.
I sit in my balcony
day in and out,
waiting for you
to come back to me.
But you,
you never do. So now,
I've stopped sitting in my balcony.
I rather sit in my room,
all by myself and sip a cup

of hot milk just as you liked it
When the main door slightly
creaks open;
I stand ready;
with the knife in my hand
when I hear a little meow.
And there you were–my baby, my kitten.

- kc

I met Kavya, just once. I am a 22 year old college graduate who works with educational organizations to bridge exposure gap in India. Once I attended an Open Mic story-telling gathering at KunZum Café, Hauz Khas. Out of nowhere, I saw a girl dressed up in a white Kurti and jeans very boldly sharing a story that shaped her emotions. This person was so inspiring that all of us kept clapping. It's these stories that compel you to lend an ear and leave you with goosebumps. That day I shared my Facebook profile with her and recorded her video. She was the "Inspiration of the Month" for us.

Many young individuals like Kavya are gems of art, creativity and expression of good thoughts. I request and wish that we collect Kavya's writings and poetry and share it more amongst each other. Trust me when you read with your heart, there's a sense of inspiration she still reflects through this medium. Thank you Kavya.

And, a big thank you to each one of us for keeping her alive. Body is just a medium which is time bound, Kavya lives in our hearts through her art."

Ashutosh

Nostalgic Silence

He kisses me
and I,
I smell cigarettes
and then, I smell you.
He breathes heavily on my nape,
but no, I don't get those
goosebumps like I used to,
with you.
He pulls me closer
just like you used to.
And God, how I wish, but, no,
it doesn't feel like it used to.
When you'd wrap your arms around
me and make me feel like home.
He tells me he loves me;
I know, he does
and I love him too
but am I in love with him?
They say when you have to
question it–you don't, really.
He touches me,
and I let him,
You know why?
Because I imagine you instead of him.

He keeps asking me to talk more;
just like you used to.
But all I have left to talk about
is you–so tell me, what do I do?
He hugs me and I sniff him.
Why? Because I hope to smell you.
But no, I never do.
We lay next to each other
Silently; but not comfortably.
The silence with him doesn't do
the talking like it used to,
with you.

- kc

To be honest, I don't really know where to begin with. Kavya was way more than I could possibly describe and I don't really know if my words will be able to do justice to her memories.

She was the bravest person I had ever come across. She was fearless. She had been through a lot in life, and yet it never stopped her. In fact, she accepted it all and wore it like an armor and fought.

Usually, people become bitter and cynical when life treats them unfairly. But that wasn't the case with her. She instead wanted the world to be a better place and she definitely had the strength to change it. That is what I loved about her, and that inspired me; I wanted to be as strong as she was.

I am an Atheist. But her death makes me hope that I am wrong about it, that she is still somehow watching over us. She taught me a lot and to this day I try to be a better person. I try to stand up for the things she believed in, hoping to be the person that she would have wanted me to be.

Rudraaksh

My moon, my forever

I look at the sky,
and then I look into your eyes.
And ask myself,
"Is this how one is supposed to know;
whether or not they're the one
for them?"
"Is this how it's supposed to feel?
Like pouring maple syrup on a pancake
while a hurricane goes on in your insides?"
"Maybe, just maybe, you really were,
my moon. And now that I've lost you,
I'll use street lights to guide me back home."
We planned so much for the future.
Maybe, we shouldn't have.
Why? Because now,
I can't see a future without you in it.
I was a firm believer of 'forever's,
But now, I can barely picture a tomorrow.
A tomorrow without you seem dark and alone;
the same way I feel when I smoke in my room,
all alone, in the dark.
A tomorrow seems so far off, let alone a forever.
I have stopped eating my meals.
And all day long, all I do is think of you.

Wonder whether or not you think of me too.
I have a zillion errands to run through the day
and even though, you top the list,
you're the last thing I do.
No, not because I don't already think of you,
all day long. Only because I tell myself,
it will be okay by the end of the day.
But my beautiful man? It never really is.
I'm never really okay, without you, without the moon.
The street lamps in Delhi flicker and don't work.
So tell me, who is supposed to guide me,
when there is no light around me?
So let me tell you this,
and please, hammer it down your head
–you'd always be my moon.
You'd always be my forever.

- kc

Oceans

Yes, that's how silent it is,
when the two of us are together.
There are oceans
of emotional distance between us;
even though,
you sleep right next to me.
I don't know how to tell you
–tell you that I know.
I know you are seeing someone new;
and you don't love me
the same way anymore.
Nor do I expect you to.
But please know,
I'd rather lose you to
someone you're happy with
than eat on the same table
with you and feel oceans of
distance between us.
Do you remember the promises we made?
That time when you said,
you'd stay forever?
Well, how naïve was
I to not know
that a 'forever' ends this soon.

I promised to cross as many mountains
as it took to get to you.

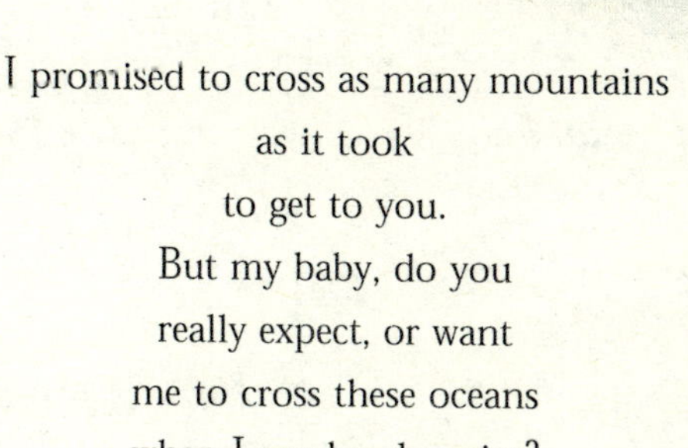

I promised to cross as many mountains
as it took
to get to you.
But my baby, do you
really expect, or want
me to cross these oceans
when I can barely swim?

Oceans... *pen drop*

- kc

Your mother, was my teacher when I was a young girl in school. It was the beginning of a relationship that I would linger onto for memories and cherish forever. You were the seed, she nurtured in all of us at school, long before you sprouted.

I never got to meet you in person. But through stories that have now become questions without answers, I will forever search for meaningful conversations that I would have loved to have with you. Perhaps some things should be left unspoken. Perhaps you would have spoken about me through your poetry someday, but you chose to become one.

We never met. But I have always known you Mishti. Like that winter sun I feel every bit of, on a hot summer day. You will always live in my heart.

Astha

4

Sleepless nights;
stained sheets.
4 in the morning;
and I take tiny peeks.

Over the almirah,
and under my bed.
I keep looking
without a tear being shed.

You're the ghost of my past,
couldn't let you ruin my beautiful future.
But what can I do,
when you haunt me,
by just saying my name
in a whisper?

I try so hard
to forget that you even exist.
But each time I see something tall and dark,
I'm reminded of the tragic echo that persists.

- kc

None

There's none quite like you,
from dusk
till dawn
you're on your toes
just to give us all the warmth.

We're not easy to take,
but when have you ever complained
giving us your share of cake,
though *ammachi* tells me
it's your buds' favorite taste.

We're all that we are,
only because you are.
No, there's none like you,
none that can make me whole
from only a few.

- kc

Dear Kavya, it's been quite a while since you last spoke to me. I have so much to tell you. I've quite some updates and I'm sure you do, too. When you left, I looked through some of our last conversations. They were mostly me telling you how beautiful you looked. I will always remember the first memory of us. The school had gotten over and your class was on the third floor. Like the weirdest child in history, I walked up to you and introduced myself. I remember telling you how I'd like to be friends with you. That was by far the most precious first-impression that I've ever formed. I need you to know that I associate magic with you. I really need you to remember that. Only magic will help me keep you in my life and I can't have it in any other way. You'll always be my younger sister and I'll always look out for you. You're too dynamic a soul to not exist anymore and I will never believe otherwise. I'm aware that our friendship was left incomplete but I'll always try to find love and closure in that incompleteness. Your didi is very proud of you. I know that you're doing something, somewhere and I know you're being kind. I promise to be kinder for you. Also, let me know if you want to chat on G-talk. Also, remember that our tiny secrets are still ours. I have them safe.

I love you. I always will. Stay in my heart, always.

Vagmi

My smile, my armour

It's never too easy,
I don't think it will ever be.
We all have a story to tell,
a lie;
to mask our true selves.

Running away,
at the pace of 1200 km per hour.
Far, far behind,
leaving the past
which was always at par.

I might reach my breaking point;
and I might not want to go any further.
But just as you have your power,
I have mine.
My smile, my armour.

- kc

AMITY INTERNATIONAL
MODEL UNITED NATIONS 2014
KAVYA
FEAR OF
FAILURE
CAN'T BE
BIGGER
THAN
YOUR
DREAMS

There's a very short story by David Foster Wallace which goes like this–There are these two young fishes swimming along and they happen to meet an older fish swimming the other way, who nods at them and says "Morning, boys. How's the water?" And the two young fishes swim on for a bit, and then eventually one of them looks over at the other and goes "What the hell is water?"

Whenever I spent time with Kavya, I felt like the young fish discovering what water is. I would always walk away learning a bit more about myself.

Around her, I was not worried about hiding my scars, I was comfortable in my skin. I believe it was because she never felt guilty about her own scars, she was brave enough to accept her vulnerabilities, and kind enough to give space to people around her to accept theirs.

It was almost as if she was saying to everyone who came across her, "It's okay, you can be human for a while, and I'd still appreciate you." I will always be grateful to Kavya for that.

Shikhar

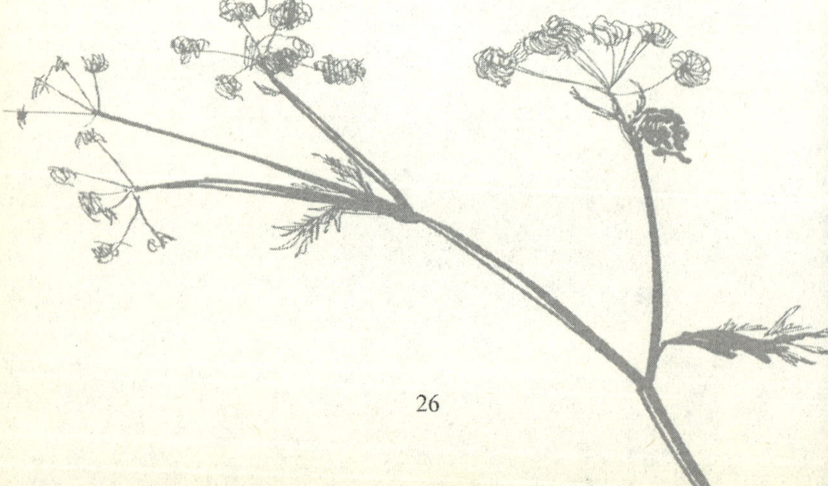

Him

The warmth of the sun,
on a -2 degrees Sunday.
Or the chill of an orange bar,
on a summer day.

The laughter of the little boy,
you sticked your tongue out to.
Or the kindness,
in that stranger's smile.

The comfort of your father's
oversized jumper.
Or the glory,
from your first win.

The rustle of the leaves,
on a late autumn afternoon.
Or the chirrup of the birds,
during an evening of spring.

The smell of chai
on a stressful day,
Or the joy of running your fingers,
over the lush pages of your book.

It's him,
through the all-of-this
and the all-of-that,
it has always been him.

- kc

Mishti was not just my little cousin, but she was also my little sister. The fondest memories I have of India, growing up all had her in them. When we were younger we would always play games together like hide and seek around the house or play games on her computer. Mishti always made me a part of her life and because of her, my time in India was always a blast.

I have memories from when we were much younger where she would show me her homework or she would proudly show me how good her handwriting was. As we got older, she switched from showing me her handwriting to telling me about her goals and ambitions. Her goals were always big and she could be absolutely anything she wanted to be because she was one of the brightest and smartest people I knew. Soon I started seeing her write and recite poems - I remember reading her first poem and I had tears in my eyes. Her poems and her writings were always moving and the words she wrote always came from her heart. I might live in the United States but I always felt connected to her through her poems.

What I loved most about Mishti is what a warrior she was in terms of speaking up on topics that are considered taboo. She started conversations on things that are often swept under the rug. It takes a true leader to not care what people think and stand for your beliefs. She may have been younger than me, but she has done more in her life than I will ever hope to. I aspire to be like her: brave, influential and real. The world changes for the better when a person like Mishti speaks up and influences others, but the world also weeps when a soul like her is lost.

The last memory I had with her was on the eve of New Year in 2015 in India at Radisson Blu. She was wearing the prettiest dress, her face was lit up with the brightest smile and we both held hands and danced all night long. There is not a fonder memory that I have. I will cherish this memory and all my other memories of her forever. My family and I miss her so much and there is nothing in the world that can fill the void that she has left.

Aditi

Check mate, once again

You bought me
a bouquet of roses
unaware
that I, hate bouquets,
let alone, roses.
But I, smile,
and accepted it with
all the love that I am capable of.
You bought me a bottle of wine
to celebrate my big win,
unaware
that I'd rather have chai.
You told me you love
Music, all genres.
Isn't that's what you said.
But just as I introduced you to my playlist.
I realized,
I made a big fool out of myself.
Why? Because you
meant not a single word you said.
When you said I was your sun,
you meant the moon in the
daylight– still there but,
not really, is it?

When you said I was your light
in the dark,
because I,
guide you to your path;
you meant I was the firefly
–used and forgotten.
When you said I was calming
like the waves at a seashore;
you meant, I was drowning you,
in my water.
And so;
so, you left.
And 'he' says,
"check mate, once again,
I got you down and this time,
I win, and you, lose",
But I,
I stare at him
I stare at him right in the eye.
And tell him that,
I will survive.

- kc

Yes, horrible things do happen. Happiness in the face of all that isn't the goal. Feeling the horrible and knowing that you are not going to die from those feelings is the point.

- Kavya

Hey sunshine!

I'll always remember you calling me and saying Ananyaaaaa,

I'll always remember the day you started calling me 'aunty' as a pet name.

I'll never forget the new kid in school who came in a bragged about knowing 5 languages.

I'll never forget the mechanical pencils and chocolates that you brought to school when your mom came back from official tours.

I'll always remember how just after school we used to call each other and discussed about TV serials.

I'll never forget how you looked on that annual day, wearing the ballerina skirt and dancing

I'll never forget how I used to teach you maths, science and social studies on call, then when we were in different sections.

I'll never forget our times on the football field and dressing room.

I'll never forget how you ran behind Divyansh to hit him, with one shoe on, and the other in your hand.

I'll never forget your birthday when we surprised you and went to Shipra mall to have pepperoni pizza.

I'll never forget how you supported me in Manesar when I felt lonely.

I'll never forget you, me and Arunima eating together and having amazinggg conversations.

I'll never forget the day when you came home just because your home was locked and you had to use the washroom.

I'll never forget when you came home, just to give me a hug and congratulate me for my college selection.

I'll always remember the way you smelled, so sweet.

I'll always remember the way you smiled, that beautiful smile.

I'll always remember the way you laughed, uncontrollably.

I'll always remember your hug. Even though I am taller, they felt so comforting.

The thing is Kavya, I love you and I'll never forget you.

Ananya

SHUSH

"I asked if you could hear me
but none of you answered.
Probably because no sound
came out of my mouth.
But would you have listened
if I did actually speak it out loud?

My father died
when I was only nine.
And to shush
is what I had always been taught
since that time.

Chaterjee Uncle,
the one uncle who gave me
a whole lot of memories;
memories to cherish,
memories to cry over.
But memories that are responsible
for who I am today.

With a box of finely packed chom-chom,
he'd come over
and pull me playfully

into his lap.
A bright pink ribbon
would always be tied on it's top.
And I'd excitedly rip it open
and dive into the box.
And my uncle would do the same,
only, for him,
the box was replaced by me.

I told him not to do it.
I told him it hurts.
But you know what he said to me instead?
Put your index on those lips
and shush while I kiss.
And so, I shushed.

I told ma
what was happening to my body.
I told her;
I don't like any of it.
But you know what she said to me instead?
Your body is not yours, but theirs;
so please them.
For this is all you can do
for as long as you are;
and never speak of it to anyone again, shush;
and so, I shushed.

Eight years later,
I was in an abusive relationship with my lover,
who would exploit me for all my skin;
in the name of love
until all that was left were mere bones.
I would ask him to stop,
tell him I am bleeding and sick,
tell him life fucked me over a million times.
And I came to you for help.
But you,
fucked me more instead.
But despite all that,
do you know what he said to me?
I am only making love to you
and even though you think
you don't like it now,
you will,
so, shush, little darling.

But this time,
I choose not to.

- kc

Mishti is a loving and beautiful child. She is with us in this world.

Madhu

Dear Bapi

Dear Bapi,
where are you?
You promised me,
you should have been home by now.
Where are you, Bapi?

Dear Bapi,
I still listen to Kishore Kumar,
hoping you'd come dancing into my room,
day after day.
I still wait for you, Bapi.

Dear Bapi,
you'd hate it when I would bite my nails.
I haven't stopped biting them yet,
I don't think I ever will.
When will you come scold me for the same, Bapi?

Dear Bapi,
you promised to take out all second Saturdays for us.
It's been 103 of those since then,
and I still have my white sun dress, pink hat and shades ready
and packed.
Are you ever going to come, Bapi?

Dear Bapi,
I suck at math
and so does ma.
I wish you would've taught me decimal division before you left;
Will you teach me now, Bapi?

Dear Bapi,
you kept telling me to embrace myself.
You kept telling me the beauty of the underlying and the unseen.
You taught me to accept myself.
You told me the society makes norms,
and I, your daughter, am there to break them.
I never understood all that then
but I do now,
So will you come and give me a hug for that, Bapi?

Dear Bapi
I loved those plastic playhouses.
And you,
You'd love building them up with me.
But now, I've packed and stored them in the closet.
When will you get it out of there and
build it back up with me, Bapi?

Dear Bapi,
You promised to protect me when I'd be in situations.
I've been in and out of trouble.
I've been through all that a girl my age shouldn't have.
How much more do I have to see, be and suffer from
–for you to come and save me, Bapi?

Dear Bapi,
you left me when I was just 9.
And as I write this,
I am double of what I was.
It has been so long;
but when will it be long enough,
for you to come back to me, Bapi?

- kc

A bright, young, smart and bold young girl with dreams in her eyes is how I remember her. Though I have never interacted with her, have read some of her poems which reflected her deep intellect.

Prema

Rehan

My younger brother;
Rehan,
would tickle me a lot.
And I would ask him to stop;
but he never did.

Whenever Abbu got us candies,
he made sure that we get an equal share.
But my younger brother;
Rehan,
would always steal mine.
I would ask to not do it;
but he, never listened.

I was the elder sister;
always taught to compromise;
to forgive and forget.
Because he is my baby brother;
and so,
allowed to make mistakes.

I remember owning a yellow salwar.
But my younger brother,
Rehan,
loved the colour yellow;

so he tore it apart.
Ammi and Abbu ignored it;
saying he is only a baby.
And babies don't mean any harm.
I'd still try,
and tell him not to tear my clothes in public;
but he, never cared.

When he was in college,
everyone in the neighbourhood
would complain to us.
They'd tell Ammi and Abbu,
"Your son whistles at each girl who passes by;
teases all of our daughters.
Ask him to stop or we will tell the police",
Ammi would pull him by his ears;
while Abbu tried to stop her
and continued to pamper him.
My younger brother,
Rehan,
did not respect me.
Nevertheless, I tried to teach him;
teach him he's wrong.
But he, he never learned.

Ammi and Abbu always wanted a son.
I, khaami, as my name suggests
was only a mistake.

So when they finally had a son;
they overlooked all his flaws.
In fact, taught him that girls are weak
and to guide them;
is a real man's duty.
Soon guide was synonymous to dominate.
And my younger brother;
Rehan,
was married off.

His wife and he
would have regular fights
always ending the same way.
Mariam bhabhi with a swollen, red face
and my younger brother,
Rehan,
completely drunk, screwing his broken wife all those nights.
Mariam would ask Ammi to help her;
but she instead would tell her,
"This is the fate of a woman".
So Mariam came to me;
and I tried to talk to my brother.
But he, never paid any heed.

Now, all these years later;
when I see Ammi and Abbu crying
as I read the newspaper's headline;
with his name in bold black letters,

attached to the word that means
so much worse than an uncultured beast
– a rapist, is what they call him;
I am not shocked.
Because wasn't it them
by whose
consent he always mocked?"

- kc

Kavya and I were friends for 6 years. Our bond wasn't constant all through these years but nothing felt different whenever we met. My school life wouldn't be complete without her. She used to sit beside while I worked on my art projects and I used to sit and watch her practice football. It didn't matter if we didn't completely understand what was happening. Being in the presence of each other and being there for each other was good enough. I always admired her for her spunk and the boldness she carried to speak her mind. She was the strongest person I knew. There was never a dull moment with her, we've fallen off chairs laughing, cooked each other food and so many countless memories. After all, she was the first person I called my best friend and who showed me how beautiful friendship can be.

Gaurvi

My Mira, bye Mira

I watch Mira
as she colours her lip,
with a shade that
looks darker than beige
but I bet,
tastes like berry.
I watch Mira as she
places that big black
bindi right between those
two perfectly arched brows
and asks me with her eyes
wide open,
"OK na?".
And I, shake my head in
disbelief at her beauty
as I realise I need to
nod. And so, I do.
I watch Mira as she
holds her dupatta
and ensures it falls
smoothly, flowing from
her shoulder through
her waist, rubbing her
hip as she moves around.
I watch Mira as she

sprinkles a pink coloured
scent on her wrist.
But as she smears it on
her thin, long neck,
it suddenly smells
like petrichor.
I imagine her
to be the soil
and the perfume liquid
to be the rain.
I watch Mira as she
decides between two heavy
gold jhumkas to go
with her orange
salwar kameez and finally,
settles on a silver one
which I bought her on Eid.
I watch Mira as she
watches herself in that mirror
which fails to capture her
elegance and depth even after
so many attempts.
The sun rays begin to hit the
windows in the room and reflect
it's sharp yet dim light
on her skin and she, she glows.
I watch Mira as she
continues to set new standards

of artistry and exquisiteness.
And I think to myself,
"Mira, my all time best friend,
would you ever be mine?"
And suddenly Ammi enters my room
and shouts at me,
"Ladke wale neeche intezar kar
rahe hain tumhara, jaldi chalo".
I look at her for one last time;
and whisper to myself as I hug
her goodbye,
"My Mira, bye Mira".

- kc

She was a sweet girl, Mishti. So appropriately named by her parents. We lived miles apart--she in Ghaziabad and I in Gurgaon. But every time we met, I was struck by the exuberance of life in her. A lovely-looking bright- eyed kid, she was unique.

It was always a pleasure to talk to her. There was a bubbling sense of life in her. Whatever she did was done to perfection, be it academics or dramatics or the other extracurricular activities she took part in. But what I will always remember her for, are the heart-touching poem she has written about her father whom she lost at a very early age.

And one day she was gone. No farewell words were spoken. There was no time to say goodbye. A beautiful flower that wilted so early. But I am wrong. She has not wilted. She is blooming somewhere else in richer colours spreading a sweeter perfume. After all, her name is Mishti!

Sengupta ma'am

Dr. (Mrs.) S. Sengupta

Juno

I was bargaining with the shopkeeper
when you walked
into my frame of reference.
And for the first time in ages, I could finally focus on one thing at a time.
You, it was you.
I could look at you for hours;
and nothing could distract me.

Hi, I have anxiety
and I can never think clearly.
But with you,
I suddenly could.
You asked me my name;
and I introduced myself as Kane;
but then I bit my lip,
and scolded myself a bit,
"Oh no, not so quick!"

I can never seem to stick
my mind to one thing
and I was so sure
you'd never talk to me again now.
So I stood there
fidgeting my fingers,

knowing the words that came out of your mouth
were to be no.
But then you held out your hand and said,
"Hi, I'm Juno".

Your hair was like the beach.
When the dim light of the setting sun fell on its sand;
–a little rust mixed with a lot of blonde.
Your eyes were like the sea at night;
very blue but so dark.
So dark that you'd confuse it with black.
Your skin was like porcelain,
only with little dots on it replaced by freckles.
Which I was dying to run my fingers over.
And your voice was the summer rain for the lifeless,
dying plants that would wash away
all the dry and bring back life.

It was funny how the sound of your voice
could calm down all the noise.
Half of them saying yes;
and half of them no;
it was always so tough
to win the battle between both.

When we went out on our first date;
I asked for a tea
but changed that to a coffee.

Then, a tea.
Then, a coffee.
Then, a tea.
Then, a coffee.
Tea, coffee, tea, coffee,
coffee, tea, coffee, coffee, tea.
I decided on the tea.
I thought you'd think
"What a creep!"
and leave.

But instead,
those rosy tender lips
curved across your face
to form a smile.
A beautiful smile;
the most beautiful I had ever seen.
You said I was funny;
I said you were the first.
The first to say that.
The first to settle all the ruffle in my head.

When we kissed,
I was unsure where to place my hands.
Since my fingers
wanted to touch all of you at once.
So I kept shifting from your waist
to your back,

to your neck,
to your chin,
to your waist,
to your back.

I was scared you'd hate our first kiss.
But instead,
those big blue eyes gleamed at me with joy as your chirpy voice said to me,
"I feel so loved, everywhere, all at once
only because of you."

I could never take a call,
never mind if we were out eating and shopping
or at home,
just by each other,
I could never take a call.

You said you liked my impulsive behavior;
but soon my impulsiveness became
a bit 'too much' for you;
which gradually changed into an indecisiveness.
A lack of ability to take a call.
A lack of firmness or purpose.
And so,
you left.

5 years later,
I leave for work at 6 AM,

and leave work by 5 PM.
I enter this café.
I grab a chair.
And I take a sip of the black tea which I've ordered
all in the same way that I've been doing
for the about 1414 days.
And I think I am recovering now.

- kc

The girl in the mirror

They asked me
what's my favourite place?
Where I
am most comfortable in?
I tell them a 4×8 sized room
–a room with tiny holes
in its sides:
From where,
rays of sunshine
come in bits and pieces,
and mix
with the scars on my skin
and blemishes;
that are looked upon
as conventionally ugly.
Making me comfortable
with the freckles
and the bruises;
bruises from self-harm
for I have hated myself
for far too long.
I cursed myself
for I never fit the beauty norms
set by our society.
Day after day,

I felt the real me slipping away.
But this room;
this 4×8 sized room
–my cupboard;
makes me feel like myself.
Makes me feel like I belong.
Makes me aware that in these scars,
lies my story and my strength.
Makes me believe
that I am so much more
than the girl in the mirror.

- kc

Writers are peculiar. Nobody seems to understand what they do, what their mind goes through. I myself, after reading so much, have never understood what circumstances one has to go through to write what some people write.

Kavya was a beautiful writer. I used to read her poetry, listen to her spoken word with envy, wondering when I could ever write the way she did. We weren't very close friends and I was slightly embarrassed to ask but once in school, I did anyway, I asked her what her 'process' was, I told her I used to write too but stopped and then never started again. She looked at me as if I had asked something absurd (maybe I had) and she told me simply, there's no process. I write what I feel, she told me. I knew that, "sure you write what you feel but how do you put it into words?" I thought but then kept it to myself.

But it is when you read more of her poetry that you know she really does just write what she feels. Her poems are simple and raw and when you read them, you know what she went through, and you feel it too. You feel calm and content and you feel happy and you feel hurt, to make someone go through all those emotions is not easy. I envy her for that, but more than that I look up to her (some might say that both are the same things) and today, now that she is not here with us, I can still read her words and feel a rush of calm, joy, sorrow, I can feel every emotion she went through when she wrote what she has written. I used to be curious of the circumstances she wrote them in, but not anymore. Why do the circumstances matter when the poet can make you feel everything that she herself felt? That, I now have realised, is enough.

Gauri

Kitchen-kitchen

At the age of 5,
I loved playing kitchen-kitchen.
Never knew
I'd feel stifled
when asked to play the same and more
for an eternity.

- kc

Bright, young and immensely gifted writer, Kavya Chakraborty left behind a void in our hearts through her sad and untimely departure. But she lives, she smiles, she speaks, she triumphs through her poetry. With a haunting personal voice, each poem becomes alive with her deep, original and exceptionally bold expressions. The range of her feelings, genuineness of emotions and rich abundance of thought enables the reader to instantaneously connect with her art. She glows like a lamp illuminating the dark spaces and shines like a star. This collection of poetry is a testimony to her enigmatic brilliance and artistic genius.

Garima

F for

F for face,
your face.
So beautiful,
so kind.
Kind enough to say,
"Keep the change".
Kind enough to say,
"Pick the dress of the highest range".

F for fancy.
You took me to a fancy place.
I loved the food
and between all of that
I started loving you too.

F for fame.
You said you didn't care about any.
Then why, I think now,
were you so full of yourself?

F for fishing.
Remember that day,
when I caught 10 fishes at the bay?
You said I was smart,
and I smiled.

So smart,
I couldn't even see beyond those lies.
I was a mere catch to you,
just like those fishes to me.

F for foolish.
I,
I am foolish.
When you asked me,
"Come over, rest here, I promise it's safe"
Why did I not use my head?
You made a fool out of me.

F for forced.
You, yes, you.
You forced me.
I told you I don't like it.
I told you I don't want you to touch me,
but you, forced me.

F for fighter.
You fight,
I clap.
And then
think to myself,
"what a strong man!".
But this time,
I swear,
I put up a fight too.

F for fuck.
You fucked me.
I was fucked by you.
No, I didn't want you to,
but when have you ever listened?

F for free.
I ask you to let me go now,
but you tell me
"you are a woman and so,
you're bound to be a sex slave"
and so, I was never freed.

F for Fatimah.
Hi, I am Fatimah
or rather,
was.
But you
can still find me
at the address of my God.

- kc

You are Beautiful
Amazingly Talanted
Come on Wake up it's
a new day.
HUG MOM & BHAI
YOU
CAN
DO
KAVYA!
YOU'RE WORTH OF SO
MUCH MORE
LET'S MAKE
LIFE
A BETTER
TO LIVE

Kavya Chakraborty , the name says it all.
A girl with so many adventurous desires, talent and exclusive uniqueness in her personality.

I met her two years ago in my tuition batch and was surprised to see such a unique personality at such a young age.

She was simply blessed with words and thoughts; she created magic with words. No one knew that she will write magic. I still remember her poem ' dear bapi' which she wrote for her father. Even her Instagram captions are full of magical words.

No doubt, she was a bright, intelligent student with super sharp mind but her interests span far more than academics. She was driven by her fascination with adventures and philosophy.

She never dressed up for society, not falling into any culture or category of personality decided by her skirt or her jeans.

She was unlabelled, uncategorized, raw and honest.

Now you know what was unique about her.

It takes lots of courage to bear the pains she had experienced. A soft hearted girl had seen many worst phases of life but still used to give a gentle smile every time our eyes met.
She was a warrior for every person who knew her.

We shared conversations casually during our tuition classes and suddenly I felt from tuition classes to my home study mate, she became one of my closest friends.

I never knew she would mean so much to me and I would end up losing her but the truth be told, she's gonna stay forever in my heart. As you know, a person may die but her words can never ever die. Words are immortal and Kavya has left a deep imprint on our hearts that nobody can ever forget her.

Riya

They will kill you too

We have balloons,
rainbows and
cotton candies.

We have so much to offer
than you'd even ask for.
You will love the flavours
of ice cream
which we have in variety.
You will love the soft shower
which makes it indistinguishable
to figure out whether you've cried
or otherwise.

We have so much to offer;
but most of all,
we have opinions,
and judgments,
and stares,
and can easily play
the blame game.
Tell us your pick,
and we
can serve you on a plate.

At age 10,
we will shame you
for interacting too much
with the boys of your colony.

At age 14,
we will stare at you
up and down
and make you feel uncomfortable
for clothes you thought
were your size.

At age 17,
we will teach you to say no
but when you say it
we will forget the entire concept
of consent.

When I write this,
it's more to warn you
than welcome.
Because I know,
this place does not
plant the seeds of freedom.

So remember,
remember all of this
before you decide
to plant yourself

in my womb.
Remember,
that if,
just in case,
you are a woman,
they will kill you too.

- kc

Kavya was one of the featured artists at our open mic event 'Lights, Camera, Words! 2.0' and within the span of her 5 minute performance she managed to touch over 300 hearts that day. We are proud to have been a part of her life and we are grateful to her for bringing her charming personality and her beautifully woven together words into our lives.

Meraki: The English Literary Society of
Sri Guru Gobind Sahib College of Commerce,
University of Delhi

Nerissa

Rosie lips,
chubby cheeks,
dark brown eyes
gleaming at me
as you ask me,
if you
can go out
with your friends yet.
I let you go
but only once you promise
to be home by eight.

I stopped believing in magic
when I turned eleven.
I couldn't seem to use my wand
the same way those Disney Princess would.
But when I held you
you, a tiny creature,
so fragile;
that you could break with the wind's blow.
I decided to protect you;
protect you from all the evil,
protect you from all the immoral.
I knew there existed magic
for you were mine.

We eat fish curry;
each Saturday.
And even though I'm not too fond of it,
you do enjoy your Saturday meals
and that suffices.

You love Taylor Swift
and I,
Muhammad Rafi.
But by now,
I have adapted myself
to dance to your favourites.
And in all honesty,
for me, it completely works.

I used to hate the colour pink,
even as a kid myself.
But as I see you,
walking down the corridor
in your flurry pink dress,
I've begun to rethink my choices.

Your school is only a 5 minute walk
but I,
make sure to drop you.
"Why?" you keep asking me.
And I tell you each time,
that I am scared to lose you
in all this darkness.

I pick you up from school
each day,
every day,
exactly at 2 in the noon.
I sit in the car
as I wait for you
—wait for my Nerissa
to come running towards me.
But you,
still haven't.

- kc

Young lady with a pleasant smile,
Curly black hair,
Dark deep eyes,
Is the face I remember of Mishti. God be with her.

Neeru

Hi, my name is fear

You and I
have always been together,
best friends;
always and forever.

You look back
and I
am always at your back
pushing you
down
so you,
can get up and run afar.

Age 6
you touched a hot pan,
and since then,
never again.

In 9th,
you failed math
and after your ma's reaction,
you never let her in.

Now, as that man
covers your mouth

grabs your hair,
and drags you into his house,
you take hold
of the nearest bottle of whiskey
and kill him
when he didn't let you free.

Hi, my name is fear
and I am dead.

- kc

The memory of Kavya that I have in my mind is that of a very smart, confident and strong girl. Unfortunately, I couldn't get the opportunity to interact with her for a longer span of time but the few moments I spent with her will always remain fresh in my mind. Now that I am writing these lines, it seems to me as if she is sitting just next to me , listening to each word very patiently as she would do in the class. Kavya, I miss you but this question would always haunt me WHY?

Namrata Ma'am
(Dr. Namrata Chatterjee)

Getting there

They told me I'll be fine.
They told me it'd be over
They told me I'd get there,
sooner or later.

But they failed to let me know,
just how long the wait can be.
I've been trying so hard for years,
but looks like my wings will never be free.

I'd always sit in crowded rooms,
but never was anyone around me.
Not like I didn't have friends or I didn't like to talk,
but they'd understand only so little when I'd open my mouth.

So I'd shut my eyes and purse my lips,
and let them label me as an introvert or a shy kid.
When I walk across the halls, they'd scream "depression" as they saw me.
They laughed about it as if it was something I chose to be.

You're almost there

But they told me it'd be fine.
They told me it'd be over.
They told me I'd get there.
And I'll make it happen NOW, there is no later!

- kc

Kavya Chitti, a name given to her by me. For her, I was her baby sister. She was always protective of me with all the love, warmth and care. She had her own different ways of expressing love and care for the people she loved. My interaction with her was for a very brief period of time but the memories we made together are enough for me to cherish for the rest of my life. She taught me so much. Anyone who was lucky enough to know her closely can tell that she had a different charm altogether. She was a selfless person, and her biggest strength was writing. She gave me the strength and courage to never be afraid of being myself, to never give up, shine as the stars shine the brightest on the darkest of nights. She was and always will be very important for me because she played a very significant role in helping me grow into the woman I am today and the one I shall strive to be tomorrow. Her absence haunts me every day for I have lost not just an elder sister but a part of me. I know she is watching me from somewhere and I'll make her proud of me.

With Love
Mani

Long Distance

We've been together
for almost 4 years now
and all they ask me
is how.
You were a year senior to me,
and though you never studied your own subjects,
you'd always help me with mine,
staying up with me through all those nights.
Tons of boyfriends made,
and none of them ever stayed.
But you,
the one I friendzoned,
would be there for me
regardless of when I phoned.
We made sure to not let our differences
come in the way of our relationship.
Through different cities, states or time-zones
the strength of our bond always shone.
People kept asking us,
how do we keep up with all the distance.
And even after all the time,
I am unable to answer such questions.
A lot of people have asked me
what's my definition of the 4 lettered word.
I smile and take a step back,

and point towards you
to let them all see
–my best, best friend
who's always mistaken
for my long distance boyfriend.

- kc

I never met Mishti personally but over the past several months, I have come to know her from her mother, her Facebook posts, and her poetry. It suffices to say that she has taken permanent residence in my heart and mind. As I read her poetry and watched clips of her readings, I was impressed by her artistic talent and ability. To quote Chuck Palahniuk, "We all die. The goal isn't to live forever, the goal is to create something that will." I think Kavya (Mishti) Chakraborty, in her very short life of eighteen years, did just that and did it well. My life is forever changed and enriched by Mishti, and my only wish is that I had gotten to know this amazing young woman! Many thanks to Leena Chakraborty, Mishti's mom, for allowing me to be a part of this tribute. Leena, you are awesome and Mishti could have been no less!

Daisy

I forgive you

It's 5 in the morning.
I lay in my bed,
thinking,
thinking if we,
if we could've made it,
somehow, anyhow.
And then I think,
whether or not
you think about it too.
I slept for a few hours today,
but my eyes still feel weary.
Have you
been sleeping lately?
I keep wondering
How you're doing
and whether or not
you ask yourself
the same questions
as I do.
Was it easy for you
or are you pretending?
Do you still like tea?
or have you left it,
right after you left me?
Do you remember

all the things
I told you
or have you erased
those memories?
All the memories;
memories of
you and I?
I've been angry;
angry like the
water spilling out
of a saucer
you left to boil
and forgot
to check-up on.
Is that
what happened;
happened between
you and I?
I had made plans;
plans to catch you up
in a lone, dark street
and strangle you;
strangle you
till you accept that
it was all a plan.
That you never cared enough;
that it, wasn't true
–the love between
you and I.

But instead, I
lay in bed all day,
All night,
counting hours
as they pass by.
Hurt myself, for I,
hate myself.
Why?
Because it's not in me
to hate you.
It's 5 in the morning;
and I've lost track
of the days.
But now,
I've stopped lying,
stopped beating
myself up
over and over,
for something
that isn't even on me.
I put a saucer
filled with water
up on the stove
and watch it;
watch it as it boils.
I add tea leaves;
with 3 spoons of sugar
just as
I've always liked.

I stand in my balcony
as I sip my tea
and decide to
let things go.
Why?
Because I tie no weights
to my ankles.
And so,
I forgive you;
forgive you
not for your sake,
but mine.

- kc

Mishti most certainly was a special girl. While I did not have the fortune of meeting her in person however, I feel I know her quite well through the legacy of poems she has left behind. At her age, such profound and compassionate thoughts expressed with so much passion is exceptional. Unfortunate that she is no longer amidst us, however she would keep illuminating our life through her work. May her souls rest in peace.

Megha

Whisper

Whisper!
That's what I was told,
when I first discovered
the blood that flows
between my two legs.
Whisper!
That's what I was told
when I was bullied
by a rich boy at school.
Whisper!
That's what I was told
when I realised I wanted
to pursue higher education and be
independent because independence
was never mine to have but
my lover's.
Whisper!
that's what I was told,
when my cousin touched me
in places that were supposed to be
no one else's but mine
because if I do–who'd marry me?
Whisper!
that's what I was told
when I thought I had the freedom

to choose my lover, to say the least.
Whisper!
That's what I was told
when I found out that my supposed lover
who,
my father chose for me,
was having an affair.
Whisper!
That's what I was told;
when I was forced into bed by my
husband–but wait,
it's not really
rape because he's my father's choice.
He's allowed to do whatever.
Scream! Scream! Scream!
After 35 years of life,
13 years of a failed marriage,
and few months of single motherhood,
that's what I tell my daughter
–scream your lungs out
and let your voice be heard!

- kc

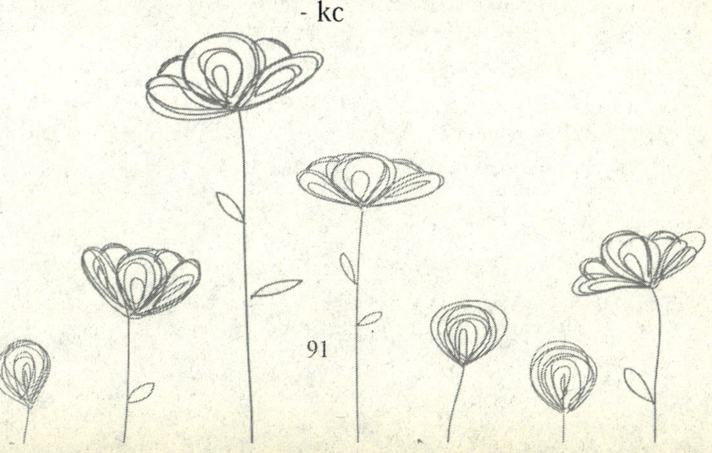

Dear Mishti,

The first time I met you was in third grade. You stood out among the group of new kids with your head full of curly hair. You seeped into my life slowly as I discovered your charming wit and your undying humour. You are so deeply intertwined with all my childhood memories that I can't remember those days without seeing your face. I remember everything; your 11th birthday when we rang all the bells in your apartment complex, the trip to Manesar in third grade, bunking classes in fifth grade, the soccer matches, the trip to Dehradun. On my 13th birthday, you told me that you love me a lot and that you can always rely on me. I assured you of the same when we turned eighteen and I hope you know that it shall be the same way for the rest of my life. You understood people better than they understood themselves probably because you felt emotions more deeply and vividly than most people. There are a lot of things I wish I could've said to you, a lot of things I wish I can say to you now but those moments are lost so the best I can do is make sure that the words you wrote are always treasured.

I miss you.
Akriti

Oh! Dear Jolene

This poem is inspired by the song Jolene....written & composed by Dolly Parton. The poem runs parallel to the song because the poet is relating the lyrics on her imagination & experiences.

Jolene, Jolene
I wouldn't beg you;
not for a man,
not for anything.
take him if you may
because if,
you can
then he's not my man
anyway.

Jolene, Jolene
you're breathtakingly gorgeous
but you know what?
So am I,
in my own ways
and there is no comparison
because neither of us
should measure ourselves
with each other's
or someone else's
scale and standard

of beauty.
We all have our different
definitions of
being beautiful,
so no,
I cannot and I wouldn't
compete with you,
Jolene.

Jolene, Jolene
my man talks about you
in his sleep
and I, couldn't,
rather, even if I could,
I wouldn't shed a tear
because I,
am enough for myself,
Jolene.
So let me tell you this:
there's nothing
that I'd do
to keep him with me;
he's all yours,
Jolene.

Jolene, Jolene,
if you intend to take my man
and you think it comes with ease;

then go ahead
and do it
because I don't need a man
to complete myself,
Jolene.

Jolene, Jolene
I wouldn't beg you;
not for a man,
not for anything.
Take him if you may
because if,
you can
then he's not my man
anyway.

Jolene, Jolene
you could have your choice of men
and so could I.
But I'd rather
neither of us
see it that way
because men
aren't objects to obtain;
no human is.
So, when, you fall
for another individual,
love and respect them,

instead of obtaining them
because
playing with emotions
is not a game,
and if it is,
then it's a sick one,
Jolene.

Jolene, Jolene
I had to have this talk with you
not because
my happiness depends on you.
But for seeing others grow,
and love and respect each other
serves my compassionate heart,
Jolene.

Jolene, Jolene
I hope you realize,
the worth of being a human
and being able to love another
because I do.
And so, I've decided
to love myself a bit more this year
and leave things;
which lack honesty and love
as deep as mine,
behind me and start new this year.
I wish you all the luck and love

but if you still want that man
I used to call mine,
feel free,
Jolene.

- kc

Kavya was quite consistent with her craft. I remember how I was so awestruck when I heard her two pieces, one about her Baba and other about Child Abuse.

What's wonderful was that they made the same impact at LCW 2.0 as well when she performed those poems again. The two times I met her, she was clad in a saree and would ask for a chair to be put near the mic to put her water bottle. It was her trademark.

At LCW 2.0 she asked me to put the chair on stage and I was like "yes, yes I know you need it!"

It was heartbreaking to know she isn't amongst us when we tried to contact her for our third open mic.

Divyanshu

Meraki The English Literary Society of SGGSCC

Hotel rooms and strangers

There is something about
hotel rooms that has
always, always comforted me.
The idea that another body;
another soul; has been to
this same, exact room;
slept on the same,
exact bed does not
terrify me. Instead, it calms
the rush of my beating heart.
It's not the same as going to
your friend's place and staying
there. Why? Because, well, you
know your friend but in hotel
rooms there lies a sense of
unfamiliarity within ease
and contentment, you know?
And even though they make
the beds again and clean the
room once you've left it;
you know for a fact that
someone else, a complete
stranger has been here

and that is exactly where I
find my solace
– in a complete stranger.
I believe strangers are who
hopes rise from.
I mean, you cannot expect
or hope much from a
person you already know,
but, a perfect stranger;
they could be all you've
been looking for. No?
And it's horribly sad how we
let that opportunity pass us
by. The opportunity to find
all your stones, stars, clouds,
songs, values, comebacks,
flowers, moon and the sun
all in one entity.
Sad, isn't it?

I say, find your hotel room
and never let it go.

- kc

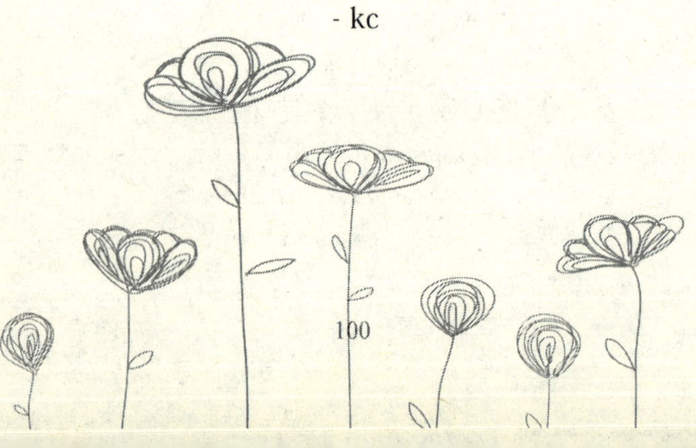

Hi Kavya,

Hope you are resting in peace and are happy. I am and have always been so proud of you as a person, as a speaker and as a human. Reading your poems, seeing you act (even if it was in front of Shivali ma'am as a surprise) and having talks like "It is so cool in a war"...we have had a real blast, from football matches to birthdays, from school hugs to hitting me when I was leaving the hostel, you saw me go through so many phases and likewise. But we were happy in what we were in. I remember scolding you like an elder sister for wasting food, for not eating your meals, for sleeping throughout the day. I remember talking to you about Harry Potter, about your super seniors, about how you shaved your head and how breezy it felt. I remember it all and will cherish it for life. I love you and you will always be in my heart. Forever.

Aastha

I do

I like your kajal
– neither does it stay
at its place nor
does it completely
wear off. It smudges
just a bit and stays
a bit more.
I do, I like your kajal.
I like your earlobes
– those silver earrings
don't look too small
or too big for it,
almost like the jeweller
specially made it to
fit your ears.
I do, I like your earlobes.
I like your nose
– how it twitches when
you're angry or trying to
control your laugh. Man,
can anyone tell the
difference but I?
I do, I like your nose.
I like your lashes
– fluttering on my arms

when you're fooling me
expecting me to believe
you're fast asleep, right
next to me.
I do, I like your lashes.
I like your laughter
– how you're the only
one laughing at all your jokes
or rather snorting like a pig
while at it and never
stopping, unless asked to.
I do, I like your laughter.
I like your tumtum
– how they hold the
capacity to eat 6 paranthas
at one go and give
absolutely anybody a
run for their money.
I do, I like your tumtum.
I like your feet
– tiny, and soft, as a petal
but unstoppable when you
hear a tune you'd like to
groove to.
I do, I like your feet.
I miss you and every Sunday,
I visit you, and wait for you, but
the rationale inside me tells

me it's an impossible wish. And
so, I leave, keeping your
favourite white lilies at my
favourite feet belonging to
my ever-so-favourite person.
I do, I miss you, a whole lot.

- kc

I met Mishti while I was working with Leena, her mother. Mishti had then recently lost her father and the family was going through so much. Mishti was shy, but had a smile that could fill the entire room! There was something so contagious about it and I fell in love with this young vibrant girl. We connected instantly. Inquisitive young thing that she was, she would want to know everything I did at work with utter fascination in her young eyes. Always trying to look for something to help her mother overcome the sadness of having lost her husband. My heart bled for her, but for a girl who should've been asking for someone to lean on, she was only trying to be a pillar of strength for her mother. My admiration for her soon turned into a friendship. Who says your friends should be of the same age?

Over the years we connected on Facebook and I would often see her uploads. Some of them surprised me. Honestly, some even shocked me, but mostly it was her lovely face that made me smile. Alas, the sadness she experienced at such a young age was a part of her and reflected in what she said in words through her poetry. Her words reflected wisdom far beyond the young teen that she was.

I hope you are in a peaceful place now dear Mishti, because that's what you were craving for, that's what we crave for you. I will always love you and miss you so very terribly."

Archana

Quite like me

They say,
"there are tons of
fishes in the pond.
But, to me,
there is none
quite like you.
They say,
"people come and go,
and that is a part of
our ever-going life",
but, to me,
there is none
quite like you.
They say,
"Letting go is the hardest
but the most beautiful
part." So, I ask them,
"What if I want to hold onto
the memories like a child
never wanting to let go
of his mother's dupatta?"
Because, to me,
there is none
quite like you.
They say,

Memories are like balloons

"memories are like balloons
– holding onto them would
never give you as much joy
as allowing them to fly high
up in the sky, far, far away from
you." So, I find myself new
balloons only to set them free
too and complete a full circle
because, in time, I realised,
there's none
quite like me.

- kc

I haven't met Kavya in person but heard about her from Leena, my friend of Narsingarh School days. We had planned to meet but somehow it didn't happen. See the irony, I was welcomed by the smiling, attractive photo of Kavya when I actually wanted to meet her. It is shattering to lose such a young budding talented child. This charming girl has left a void for all her admirers but has gifted us her poems as compensation! May Almighty bless her and rest her soul in peace.

Prema

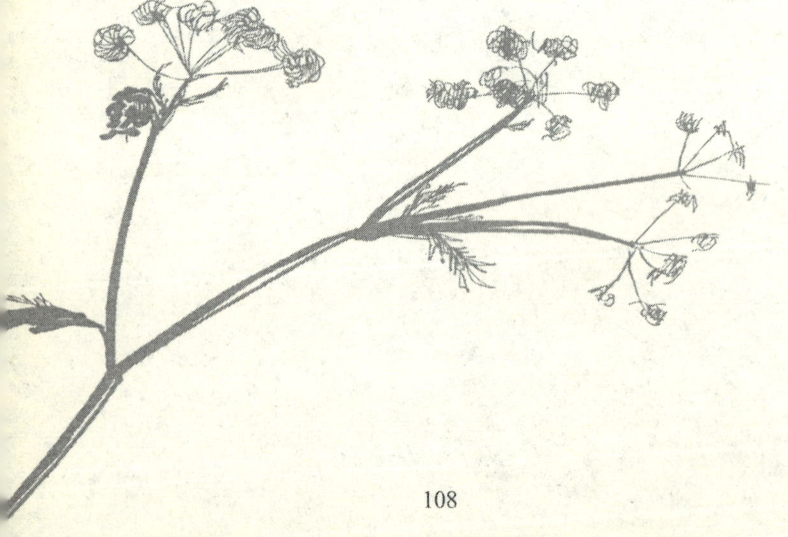

She

I'm in my room,
working on the laptop
– a laptop that
Abbu recently bought
for me as a present
because I got into
IIT Delhi, which was
more of his dream
than mine but does it
matter either way?
I was working on the
brand new laptop for
a project which had
to be submitted in
less than an hour and
usually in such scenarios
I go bonkers but this
time I didn't.
I didn't go bonkers
because I saw something
more captivating
– something that deserved
my, in fact, everyone's
attention. I see her.
I see her walking past me

in a rust coloured saree
which goes perfectly with
her skin tone. Her hair is
tied in a bun of towel which
she gently opens and then,
swiftly, brushes the towel
against her hair.
Her hair- spun out, spiral
like and stunning everyone
around her. She wears a silver
plated nose ring which blends
elegantly with her sharp
features just like rust colour
of the saree with her tanned
skin. Her hair is pure black
and once she's done brushing
it, she forgets that her hair
is still damp and that,
THAT dampness of her divine
hair leaves her blouse with
a mark of wetness and revealing
-revealing what's only a
fragment of her skin
from under the damp piece of
cloth. Allah bless that cloth!
She throws her hair back
with little droplets of
water coming right at me

– touching my face and
suddenly, I feel god-like.
She applies surma around
those big brown eyes,
confirming that the
combination of brown and
black will always be the best;
rather, anything on her would,
always, undeniably, be the best.
I am in a world of my own
when Abbu calls at me and asks
me to get three packs of milk
and as I leave, she, my Ammi
shouts from the back "ek
packet extra le aana".

- kc

Eulogy for my dearest friend Kavya

She was different from the crowd
With a cloud of black short curly hair
Covering around her face.

She was the first friend I made.
I cherish her a bunch
Although our times have been short
Yet unforgettable ones.

Words seems so feeble
in moments like this
Life is so precious
and death such a thief,

The journey of our friendship is inexpungible
Nothing was more important to her than those close
to her.

Let the memories of her put the string
back in our lead-heavy legs
take moments to laugh those tears away.

Let the warmth of her eyes and smile not dry out
Speak about her, keep her close and in our heart
Let her voice boom
Time gone was too soon

The fact that you're no longer here
will cause me pain.
But you are forever in my heart
until we meet again.

So rest in peace, free from all pains
till we meet in heaven, united again.

Manyata

You are

You're the air bubbles
– making me happy for a
while and then popping,
taking away all of my happiness.
You're the waves at the sea
– coming towards me.
As I run towards you too
but suddenly you go back;
and just as you leave
so does the rush in my heart.
You're like the balloons
– I'm content as long
as you're with me but
some days you burst
and others, you leave me
and fly high in the skies;
making me question whether
to be happy for you to be
able to reach those heights
or grieve because you're
not with me anymore.
You're all this and so much,
SO SO MUCH more than this.
So much more than words and
poetry and sunshine and

butterflies and lavenders
and everything else.
Sometimes I wonder how can
one person be both my sunshine
in the day and my moonlight
in the dark, when there are no
street lamps to show me the way?
Maybe, someday you'd stay
maybe someday you wouldn't leave
me for the happiness of a 7 year
old or to follow the natural
pattern of our universe or
in search of greater heights.
Maybe, just maybe, you'd stay
and never leave.
Maybe, just maybe, you're the
one for me. But I'd never know
unless I try.
I mean how can you know what's
at the end of the road unless
you walk all those miles?
And maybe, just maybe,
you are my destination
and finally, I'd be home.

- kc

Kavya's confidence was amazing & infectious. She was a genuine person & I still remember her whole-hearted smile. But just do not understand why her end came so soon???

Renuka ma'am
(Mrs. Renuka Seshan)

Him

You and I,
we're sleeping
– sleeping, just an
inch apart
but the distance
between us is
inversely proportional
to the distance
between him and me.
Geographically, he's
far, far away from me
but emotionally?
So close; closer than
anyone's ever been.
I can't talk to him
and you? You're either
always unavailable or
unwanted. And the one
I want or rather,
need to
talk to isn't here.
And will probably
never be. So I go out,
slide the balcony's door
open and with a black

cigarette between my lips
and tears flowing down
my cheek, light it up.
I look up at the stars
and wish
– wish that he's
looking at the same stars
just as I am and thinking
of me just as I am, of him.

- kc

I'd always seen a spark in her. She was energetic, cheerful and most importantly, expressive. It was the sudden turn of events that we realised that it was only isolation that preserved her existence. She was selective in her choices but extremely cooperative, caring and friendly with the handful of people she allowed in her life. We miss her and wish Kavya's poetries will let the readers have a glimpse of her potentials as well as understand her and her feelings better.

Indeed life is shocking, impertinent and insolent but that is how it is.

Remi ma'am
(Mrs.Remi Srivastava)

Do you?

Do you
miss me
as much as I do?
Do you?
Do you look at
the ceiling and
imagine us
under it
looking at it,
together?
Do you?
Do you still smoke
as much as you
used to
or do my thoughts
tell you not to?
Do you?
Do you look beside
yourself and when you
don't find me,
sleeping right next to
you anymore, feel
as miserable as I do?
Do you?
Do you blame me for

everything that went
wrong between us
or do you blame
yourself?
Do you?
Do you think of me
in the daylight
or only at night,
when you're all by yourself?
Do you?
Do you remember Mira
and then, remember me?
Do you?
Do you think we could've
made it and actually
survived through this?
Do you?
Do you still love me
or have you forgotten
all the time we spent
with each other?
Do you?
Because I, do.

- kc

Dear Mishti,

To you and the readers, I am your mother's ex-colleague who shared lunch spaces and later, went on to share each other's woes and happiness too. To me, you are a supremely intelligent, multi-talented and gen Y girl who had made your family so proud through your achievements...a wizard of words, sporty, tackling adolescent issues with grit and courage, that mamma's girl who often took tips on choosing a right partner, that daughter who often gave her high score to mom when she was smiling .

Bapi's little girl talking to him often at night....that girl who's accolades and laurels were often a benchmark to other students ..
You touched each and everyone around you with your vibrant self...
You are loved and missed heaps wherever you are...

Praying for your family to bounce back with all the strength...

Love,
Jayanti

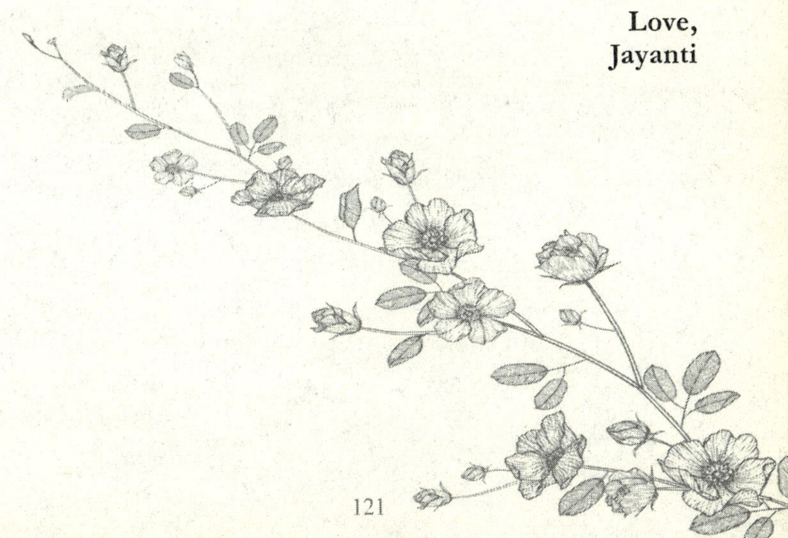

Checkmate

I was hurting
and vulnerable.
That's when I found you.
And you promised;
promised to heal me,
heal all my wounds
with showers of love
and security and warmth.
And I,
I was healing, yes.
You told me my scars,
my blood and vulnerability
makes up for my minus.
And I,
I was believing you.
You tried changing me,
changing me for the good
or rather,
for 'our' betterment'
as you'd call it.
So you'd cover my scars
and my thorns
which were partially the reason
my marks existed.
I had harmed myself

a little more
than any other individual
had been able to.
But you said,
"no, hide, change;
the world can't see you
for who, you are"
And so I,
I changed, I changed for you.
Until a day came
and you turned out
to be the best mistake
I had ever committed.
You pointed at my thorns
right at me,
passing through me
visibly trying to kill me
and said, "check mate".
And so, I bled;
a lot more than before.
I learnt it the hard way.
But guess what?
My blood is my crown now
and I, am the goddess of my own town.

- kc

I have not been able to pick the right words for you,
But here I am because you would have loved if I did.
I remember you taught me how to perform,
How to speak and where to stop the sound.
And faith and love in abundance you showered,
More than I had for myself, you empowered.
You are one of my favourite performers,
The one I spent the most crucial years of my school life with,
The one who'd adjust her specs with her right hand while talking,
And do this thing with her tongue to take pauses.
I still remember the last time I met you,
It was the last time I visited school,
In the metro, we talked about self-love and expectations,
Then, we stayed few minutes extra by the metro station,
Even though your class was in another ten,
But I am so glad, we did then,
For that was the last time I saw you.
Your hugs were the warmest,
And smile most contagious.
I remember the debate competition we went to,
You froze but it was the most fun day,
And one of the happiest memories I have of you.
It did not matter if I was elder,
You were always way mature and stronger.
I still remember the day we gathered for a group project,

But you joined and we stayed till 8pm,
8pm and being 15 kms away from home was big deal then.
But it was all worth it, I am so glad, always will be.
There were times I thought we'd never speak again,
But we did, again and again.
Someone told me,
It was your piece of art,
I must learn to appreciate it,
Even if it was a short one.
But I appreciate the artist more.
I've come to realise,
I can't write even half good as you did.
My words are all over the place,
Just like my emotions.
Also I remember my last conversation with you,
I've screenshot it incase anything happens.
I told you how sorry I was for all the times I've hurt you,
And I wanted you to know how much I cared about you,
And loved you.
And you told me,
"I know, Jyoti. I hope you know I love you immensely too."
And all I could say in return was thank you so much.
But a week and two days later,
I was sorry again.
I still am.

Jyoti

Werewolf

The werewolf comes.
Hush!
I hear the scraping of his feet
on the doormat.
I can't make a sound.
He'll hear me.
I look through the window on my bedroom.
The full moon. Oh, how so bright it shines,
telling me of the werewolf's arrival.
I dare not make a sound.
But he will hear me.
Oh God.
He scratches my door.
And before I know, I open it with a smile.
And there's that look in his eyes,
those red eyes.
The eyes that enchant me everytime I stare into them.
He bites my neck
and my body loses its stiffness.
It's warm poison runs through my body.
Oh but this werewolf, you, yes you are my love.
You return every full moon and I open my door for you.
Just for you to leave the next morning, leaving me to wait

for another full moon.
Leaving me to wait for my werewolf.

- kc

Your presence was like a light and joy
A beautiful soul who was very coy

You taught us all to do our best
to in the moment live
to never hold a grudge for long
And to always give

We will remember you forever
For you, our hearts will always have room
We loved you more than you will ever know
You left us way too soon!

Amit

Disgrace

We hurry to the police station
the officers lodge an FIR case
for another rape that took place.
They ask me my name
and I point towards my younger brother,
so he could tell them.
Amir,
but they,
shut the log book
called him the rapist instead.
Tell us, we are a disgrace.

- kc

Dear Kavya,

It was difficult for me to write to you, once I realized that you won't read this as our 'Chakraborty'. Logic said "She won't know how much you valued her" but if I hadn't convinced myself to write this, maybe I'd have even more regrets to live with.

You know I really want to tell you all that was left unsaid between us, and we couldn't find the opportunity maybe because we got too caught up in the complexity of life and couldn't figure out much. We were determined nonetheless to become better and achieve our goals, hence becoming the best versions of ourselves. You are an inspiration to me.

I still remember exactly how you taught me the correct pronunciation of your surname and how it was different from the one ending with "-barty". Soon, it became our way of addressing each other.

When I seemed annoyed about some fest work which was not getting done or school authorities were creating unnecessary issues you'd say "Hey Deswal, what's up with your event? Can we help you with something?" And knowing that a person, as talented and helpful as you were, was there to help me whenever I needed, was a great feeling. Unlike most friends, you didn't question why I gave so much of myself to something so transient. This let me bear with a lot of drama at that time, including the VP and mid-term disaster.

Going on a random rant with you was the best part, we'd complain about everything and it worked like catharsis for us :P

We had become friends on day one and I have never found it that easy to be comfortable with someone new. I've learnt a lot from you, from having faith in one's abilities, to taking a risk and trusting others; from trying to be strong to learning when one must ask for help.

You have been the best member of my team and one of the most supportive friends. Even our opinion of the world and its troubles were alike. Thanks for being there for me when I was too lost to understand anything at all. Thanks for telling me why I should never give up on my dreams.

You are one of the people I trusted blindly, one who'd never do me wrong. Someone I could celebrate happiness with, and who'd understand my silence when things went downhill.

Remember, how we discussed casually about who out of our group of friends will leave first. Back then it was a mere joke, and now it's an irony. I'm salty about it and will always be.

I was in denial when someone broke the news to me. I said, "It's probably a prank," until I verified the same and went numb. You won't know how shocked I was, I couldn't react for 15 minutes, broke down at 2am and refused to accept it for a long time. To be honest, I still haven't.

Swadha told me how you described me to her, and it's a perfect definition! I wish I had expressed my thanks more often.

I'm sorry for not trying hard enough to ask how you were when you started drifting apart, I wish I could go back and change that. I wish I had coaxed the problem out of you when you refused to talk.

I'm sorry I was not a good friend, and didn't tell you how important you are to me. I hope someday, you'll know all of this and much more that I can't write here. Goodbye until then.

Best Regards,
Tanya

Being a Woman

I'm not sure when it all started
but I must have at least been 7.
They'd pry me with their dirty eyes
and leave me screaming and helpless in the middle of the night.

I remember asking myself a million times,
if it's that one little hole in my body that makes me so weak?
Yes, weak is the word
because that's exactly how they made me feel.
They made me feel weak by dominating and influencing the women around me,
allowing me to believe that being born a woman is my own life's tragedy.

Taking control of my spirit and soul,
telling me not to do things that make me look oh-so-bold.
For bold are the women who get raped everyday
just because they decided to lead their lives, their own way.

But I wonder,
I wonder about those women who abide by your sanskari norms.
And are fooled into being your religious and cultural dogs?
Don't they feel just as scared as I do

when they walk on the streets in complete daylight among
your 'educated youth'?

Irrelevant are the details if their clothes were still on or
thrown out,
what really does matter is their dignity
which has always and always been flogged about.

- kc

Darling Mishti Girl,
Sleep on baby, in deep slumber,
While I sing you a lullaby,
Of how much you are loved,
By even me, a passer-by.

Mumma has relayed snippets to me,
And vividly, each conversation she recalls,
Of times, you, her Darling Baby Girl,
Had made such an impact to
Family, Friends, Society and all!

You were truly made for another world,
Where Love, Justice and Deep Thoughts reign,
Where your soul is free, fluttering in the Breeze,
Where ' Bapi's Little Girl' you will always remain.

Precious Sweet Mishti,
Was it so hard for you, this earthly life?
Did the road make you weary,
Was it so full of strife?
Did days of laughter pass you by,
That everything had to end?
How dare fate can play it's part?
In our teenager's story, that none, not even Mom
could mend?

But truth is, you live on, Sweet Daughter,
In your Poetry and Prose,

At such an early age, a Warrior Princess,
Like a Phoenix you rose!
Bold and Beautiful, you truly were,
Every picture of you I gazed upon,
Tugged my heart, I swear.

Thank You for this encounter,
That we shared beyond our worlds,
An epitome of Charm, Excellence and Intellect,
So full of life, that it swallowed you whole.

Mom and your poem said,
That you waited and waited for Bapi to be back,
Then finally realized that you only were the one to get ready and pack,
Your saga was short, and you called the shots,
Today and always, we will celebrate you, Mishti,
And all the lessons, you taught.

Where there is Love, there is Life,
So ' Somewhere Beyond The Rainbow',
Where skies are blue,
We hope that you are 'Loving and Living',
With Our Maker and Your Bapi, too!!

Silver Tears and Golden
Memories,
Is all Mumma & Shrey will have to share,

But I will tell Mumma on your behalf,
That you are 'O so Happy!' way up there!
Aren't you?
In a land where there are no tears,
In a land so fair and true,
In a land where the poets gather,
Listening right now, in awe of you?

Thank You, Mishti girl,
For being Leena's most prized possession,
Signing off as her colleague,
While looking up to you in admiration.

Until we meet on the other side:

Shine on and Live in Glory!
Let down your curls,
And show off that chin!
And start writing for us this 'Other Story' !

You have escaped this world,
You are finally free,
Mumma's Precious Angel,
Forever - For all Eternity!
And Yes..
I too Love You, Mishti!

Nicola

Partition

Look at those little angels
Running around
With sticks in their hands as swords
Little did they know,
These are the weapons that cut humanitarian chords

Young girls draped in their mothers' red dupattas
Because weren't we told once
Red is the colour of love
The colour of us
Then why does everyone dead bleed red?
You're all jhoothas.

- kc

I have known Kavya for last 7-8 years, being a neighbour and her mother's friend. Mishti, as she was known by her pet name was superbly talented, very beautiful, charming and pleasant.

She was a gifted child indeed. Her untimely demise has left all of us in utter shock and disbelief. Perhaps God wants her there as much as we want her here. Nothing can compensate her loss. Perhaps we can keep her memories alive by her writings in this book.

Dr. Usha

Believe me this once

You mean a lot to me
How is that so hard to see?
Yes, we have our differences
But doesn't everyone cry over some grievances?

We try to start new every hour, every day
But it never seems to work out our way
Yes, I don't apologise enough, I know
But ma, I feel more apologetic than I'll ever show
You've got your own issues, ma, and I've got mine
But tell me, is it necessary that we fight after every line?

It may be a universal fact that your child is annoyingly egoistic
But please be aware of this as well then
Your Billi's* love for you is majestic

I'm sorry for all the days I've hurt you
And all the nights you've gone to bed crying
No, I never meant any of that
But you know, I've always been an irrational kind
I won't use it as a justification
For I know what I've done, and who I am, cannot be granted any exemption

There are days when I don't apologise out of my big, fat
wall of self-pride
But there are also times when I disappoint myself as well
So much so that I don't believe I deserve a second stride

I realise, I've done nothing except being the rotten potato
of our relationship
And I know I am probably the worst daughter
But that's not going to stop me from writing this
I suck at verbally expressing myself after our fights
And my brick face might come off to you as though I enjoy
such times
I know, ma, I've given you no reason to trust me again
But believe me this once
The sun will come out after this heavy rain.

- kc

**Mishti would get into the car, bend down and hide herself when she was around 2 years old. Her father would call out for her just before starting the car, "Mishti, where are you?"...She would meow, meow...That's how we called her "Billi".*

I remember Mishti as a "little girl" running on the 7th floor, holding her mom's hand and laughing aloud and saying, 'Let us go home fast!'

Cheerful face, innocent act, amazing human, confident and energetic Mishti will always be remembered in our every thought and prayer.

"You will always be in our hearts. Stay blessed and happy wherever you are ..."

Megha

This is a mime scripted and performed by Kavya in her school on Psychology Week in year 2017. Here it goes…

So this is a story of a young 10 year old boy, James.

And I, Kavya, am going to take you through this.

Now James here was an extremely sensitive case of autism.

James' mother was a single parent and faced a tougher time than most since she had to juggle between a lot of things at the same time.

This is one of James' usual mornings.

Previously when his mother was so caught up amidst other things that she didn't realise just how much attention her child needs to lead anywhere near a stable life.

"James? Wake up. Wake up darling. You will get late for school. Alright, alright. Just two more minutes, you should be out of the bed by then."

"Uh, uh, James, uh honey, that is not how you wear a shirt. The opening of the shirt should be front facing. Yes, that's right. Now put your left arm into the left arm of the shirt and put your right arm into the right arm of the shirt. Correct, now button it up slowly and tuck it inside your pants. And now rush to school! You will get late!"

And this is one of James' usual days at school where when James couldn't calculate clearly and thus wasn't able to solve his math problems, he was left unassisted by the teacher, and later made a mockery of by his fellow classmates.

It triggered James when the students he would rather have befriended looked down upon him and called him names. After each such day James would come back home upset and crying, throwing away everything that would come his way. His mother would rush up to him and would somehow always manage to calm him down with her motherly warmth and affection.

"James, sit down. Back straight. Lay down the napkin. Fork in your left and the knife in your right.

Uh, erm, uh, give me a minute okay? I will be right back. Mamma has to do some work and mamma will be right back with you, honey.

Little James waited and waited, but being the impatient kind he was, after a little while, he tried to eat by himself using the fork and the knife. He tried. He tried harder. He couldn't get through, but he kept on trying. He kept on trying until he reached his breaking point and started throwing things away in a fit of anger.

When James' mother came back, she witnessed the mess her child had created, but even a greater mess which was coiling up within her son. She decided from there on that she would not take the slightest thing related to her child as mild or insignificant. And that's exactly where James' life reached a turning point and changed for the better.

We all need to be sensitive towards the simple fact that all that these patients of autism require is love and affection. All that any one of us requires is love and affection. Loads and loads of it. Just full of it!

Hope the book is able to connect each one of you to Mishti/ Kavya, the way you know her.

Thank you readers!

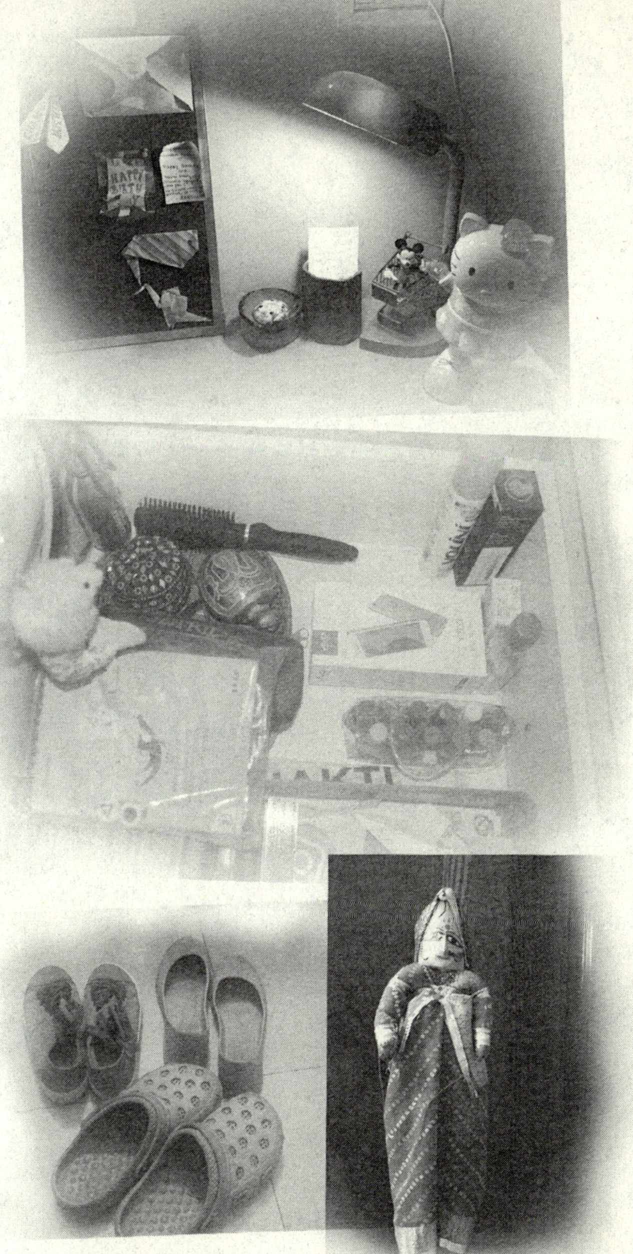